IT'S ABOUT TIME

By
**Miriam
Schlein**

Pictures by
**Leonard
Kessler**

**New York
Young Scott Books**

TICK TOCK, TICK TOCK,

hear the ticking of the clock.
Time is going by.
Where is it going?
Can you see it go by?

People say, "Time flies."
Can you see it fly through the air?

Sometimes they say, "A long time."
Is it like a long piece of string?

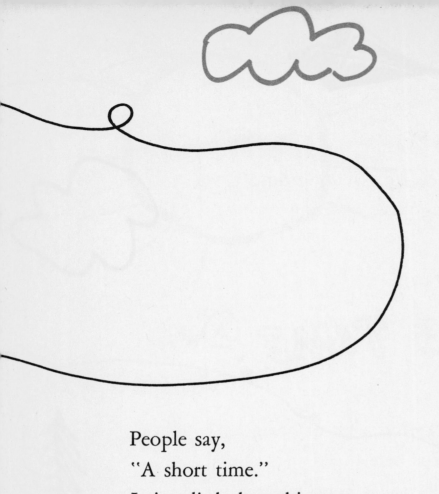

People say,
"A short time."
Is it a little low thing
that grows close to the ground?

WHAT IS TIME?

TIME is a bit of being.

It is here.

Then it is gone, forever.

TIME is—*plip*—
quick as it takes you
to wink your eye.

PLIP!

TIME is all the days
you must wait
until next summer comes.

TIME is as the moon comes up over the big dark sea.

Everything that happens
happens in a space of time—
whether it is right now
or a thousand years ago,
whether it is a little sneeze,
or a great ocean voyage
with sailors steering bravely
over the waves of the sea.

Everything that ever happens
happens in a space of TIME.

We have given names to bits of time as they pass.

Time is a second,

and longer than that is a minute,

and longer than that is an hour,

and longer than that is a day.

Time is a week;

a month.

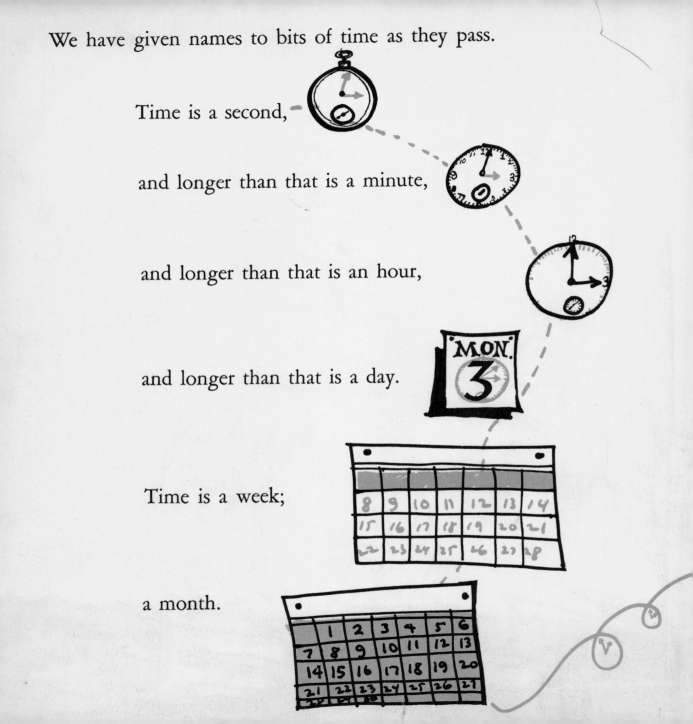

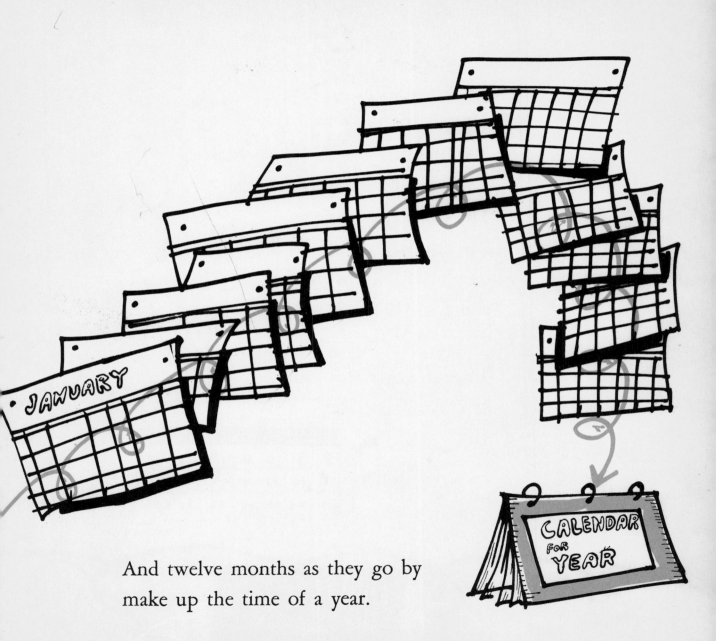

And twelve months as they go by
make up the time of a year.

Time is the minutes
just rolling along.

The clock may stop,
but time doesn't stop—
time always keeps moving
along.

You can never stop time,
or make it go faster.

Then why do people always want to know
exactly what time it is?

Very often you *have* to know
exactly what time it is.

If you're not on time
you will miss the boat;

if you don't know the time,
the train will leave
without you,

or you'll miss the first
act of the circus.

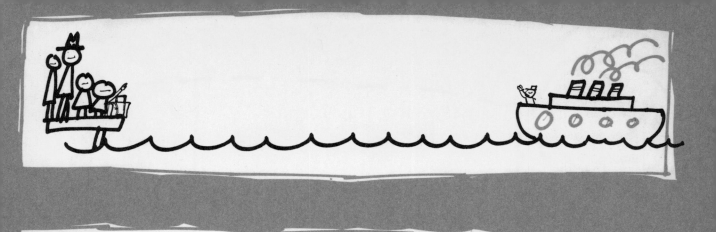

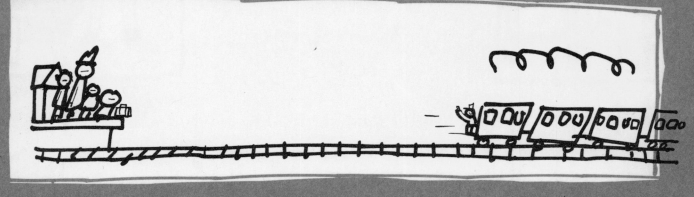

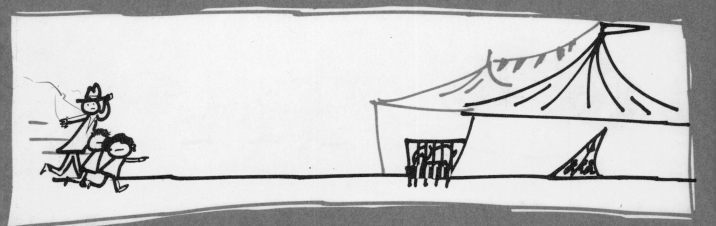

Or suppose you just
want to meet your friend.
"Will you meet me tomorrow?"
you say.

"Yes, but when?"

"When the sunlight hits the leaves
on the third branch of the tree?"

"OK, but suppose it's a cloudy day
and the sun doesn't shine at all?"

"We can meet when the fruit man
comes by with his wagon,
and stops and yells,
    "FRUIT, FRESH FRUIT!"

"Ah, but suppose the fruit man
just doesn't come that day?"

Look how easy it would be
to meet at a certain *time*.

"Let's meet at 10 o'clock."
"Ah, fine."

Because 10 o'clock will be 10 o'clock,
rainy or snowy, fruit man, or no!

How do you know when it's 10 o'clock? You can look at the clock.

When the short hand points at the 10 on the clock and the long hand points straight up to the top—then it is 10 o'clock!

Listen!

Look!

The engine goes by.

It stops.

The firemen go up the tree.

They rescue the cat!

And time has gone by. Look. The long hand on the clock has moved past 15 dots—15 minutes. One quarter of the hour has passed. Now it is a quarter past 10.

count the dots

Ah. We are 15 minutes older.

A bird flies by.

A car honks its horn.

You walk with your friend.

You talk with your friend.

And more time has gone by. The long hand of the clock has moved some more.

When the long thin hand has gone half way around, it means half of the hour has passed.

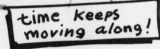

time keeps moving along!

Here comes a dog.

He's wagging his tail.

Nice dog.

He leaps up.

Right into our arms!

And now the clock looks like this ☞

The long hand has moved on to the 7. What does that mean? Five more minutes have passed. Every time the long hand on the clock moves from one number to the next, it means five minutes have passed. Five minutes more of the hour.

Anything that happens, happens within a space of time.

We go shopping.

What shall we buy?

Licorice sticks?

Candy corn?

Jelly beans? Yes!

Munch, munch.

All this time, the hands have been moving.
Now it is 11 o'clock on the dot!

No matter what you're doing,
time goes by.

Time goes by in an even way,
one o'clock, two o'clock, three o'clock, four,
each hour is 60 minutes.
Never any more or less.
It may seem like more, sometimes.
When you are waiting for something,
an hour can seem very long.

But if you are having fun
oh, a very good time,
an hour seems to pass,
whsst, just like a minute.
But it's not a minute.
It's an hour. And that is 60 minutes.

But time is not a clock.

There is time, out in the fields
where the daisies nod,
out in the woods and the wilderness,
and the animals
know that time goes by
They have no clock hanging
up in a tree,
but still, they see it get dark at night,
and they know that the day is through.
All through.
Time goes by in the woods.

Time goes by for everyone—
the king, the bee, the fish in the sea.
Time goes by.

We all share the time as it passes.

Time is the night and time is the day;
time is for work and time is for play.

And time is ever-flowing. It is like an endless river
that began back where, nobody knew.
It is all the days and years and millions of years
that ever were, long ago.

Time is right now, this minute.

And it is all the days and years
and millions of years
that ever will ever be.